Happy eighth Birthday Jenny!

Bob & Nancy, Gus, Jonna, + Phillip

The Sound
of The Bell

by Penny Anderson
illustrated by
Lydia Halverson

Published by The Dandelion House
A Division of The Child's World

for distribution by VICTOR

BOOKS a division of SP Publications, Inc.

WHEATON. ILLINOIS 60187

Offices also in
Whitby, Ontario, Canada
Amersham-on-the-Hill, Bucks, England

Published by The Dandelion House, A Division of The Child's World, Inc.
© 1983 SP Publications, Inc. All rights reserved. Printed in U.S.A.

A Book for Competent Readers.

Library of Congress Cataloging in Publication Data

Anderson, Penny S.
  The sound of the bell.

  Summary: A Vietnamese family places its trust in God
as it seeks a refugee camp to escape the war.
  [1. Refugees—Fiction.   2. Vietnam—Fiction.
3. Christian life—Fiction]   I. Halverson, Lydia, ill.
II. Title.
PZ7.A54875So   1983   [E]   83-7453
ISBN 0-89693-217-6

1 2 3 4 5 6 7 8 9 10 11 12 R 90 89 88 87 86 85 84 83

The Sound of The Bell

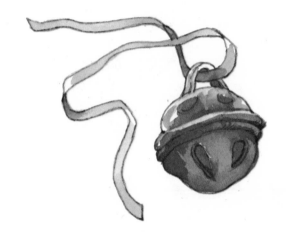

A flash of lightning split the sky. Thunder shook the small hut that was the mission school. Eight-year-old Mai bit her lip and blinked her eyes.

She looked across the room where her little brother Long sat on his bench. He was five years old but so small his feet didn't touch the floor. His brown eyes were wide with fear. His thumb was in his mouth.

Mai looked out one of the windows. The thunder sounded just like the big guns. The guns had roared for days outside the village. Mai knew the people would have to leave soon. Mai hated the war.

All day she had watched others from the country-side plod through the mud and rain. Some led oxen. Some pulled heavy carts. Some carried crying babies. Even the smallest children carried something.

For days Mama had been ready to move on. She had three small bundles waiting. They were filled with extra clothes and a little boiled rice wrapped in leaves.

Papa was already gone. He was in the hills fighting. Mai could only hope he would find them someday.

"Mai?"

Startled, Mai looked up. "Yes, Teacher."

The teacher put her hand on Mai's head. "Do not be afraid." Mai felt a tear slide down her cheek. "We must leave now. The guns are too close. Your Mama is outside with the other parents."

Mai reached out her arms to Long who ran to her. "Where can we go?" she asked.

"We will walk to the border," said Teacher. "It will be a long walk, but refugee camps are there. One will take us in. Don't be afraid. Remember, the Lord loves us. He will take care of us. No matter what happens, He is with us. Can you remember that, Mai?"

Mai nodded her head and took Long's hand.

"When you are afraid, ask the Lord to be with you and help you."

Again, Mai nodded her head.

They found Mama in the school yard. She was carrying baby Bao and all three bundles. Without saying anything, Mai and Long each took a bundle. They followed Mama out onto the muddy road. They joined the long line of refugees.

As always, Mama wore
her little brass bell. It was
pinned to her sleeve. And it
made a lovely tinkling
sound as she walked. Papa
had made the bell for her, from
an old gunshell casing he found
near the river. Mai loved the sound
of the bell. It meant that Mama was near
and that everything would be all right.

They walked for miles that first day. Mai's wet
clothes stuck to her back. The mud was ankle-deep
and cold on her bare feet. She and Long were tired
when darkness came, but they still followed Mama
and the tinkling of her bell.

It was late when the tinkling stopped.

"Mama! Why are we stopping?" Mai asked.

"I just can't go any farther tonight. I am too tired. We could lose each other in the dark. We will rest till morning."

"I am hungry," Long said.

"We can eat a little of our rice now." Mama unrolled a leaf. "But we must save some. Who knows how long we will be on the road?"

She gave a little of the rice to Long and Mai. And she put a few grains into baby Bao's mouth. But he did not want rice. Baby Bao wanted milk, but there was none.

Long ate his rice in one gulp. Then he watched as Mai ate hers—a grain at a time.

The family shivered in their wet clothes and curled up together to keep warm. They were so tired they fell asleep at once. The heavy guns did not wake them. Neither did the hundreds of refugees tramping past on their way to the border.

A long time later Mai rubbed her eyes and sat up. It was time to move on. The rain was over.

When they reached the road, the early morning sun shone on the puddles. The crowd of refugees seemed larger than the day before. Baby Bao fussed and cried. The family struggled along in the crowd, trying to stay together.

"Hang onto me," Mama told Long. "And, Mai, you stay close. Let's not let the crowd separate us. People are going in many directions. We might have a hard time finding each other."

"If I can't see you, I can hear the bell," Mai answered.

"Stay close," Mama warned again. "Hang onto me, Long."

The crowd surged around them. Long dragged his feet and hung back. "I'm tired. I can't walk anymore." He sat down in the road.

"You can't stop now!" Mai tried to pull him to his feet.

Long shook his head. "I can't walk anymore."

"Here, take my bundle, and I'll carry you piggyback," Mai said. She crouched. As she did, the crowd surged between Mama and her. Mai could hear Mama calling, and she could hear the bell tinkling. But now she couldn't see Mama.

Long climbed onto Mai's back. Mai stumbled to her feet and moved on with the crowd. She called, "Mama! Mama!" But she received no answer. And she could not hear the bell. Mama was lost in the crowd of people.

"We've lost her, Long. We've lost her. . . ."

Long cried and clung to Mai's back as she tried to push through the crowd.

"Mai?"

"Yes, Long?"

"Will we find Mama and baby Bao?"

"Yes. They can't be far away. Listen for the bell. We will find them."

"How?"

"I don't know, but we will find them."

"You are just saying that."

"No, I'm not! Teacher told me that God will help us if we ask Him. I'll ask Him to help us find Mama."

"I'll ask Him too," Long replied. He stopped crying.

Mai pushed ahead. The crowd pressed against her. She stumbled and almost fell.

"Put that boy down! He can walk as well as you!"

Mai turned to face a bent old woman. "He's tired."

"So is everyone else. You can't carry all of us." She spoke to Long. "Get down! Shame on you! You

are big enough to walk.'' She waved the heavy stick she used as a cane.

''He's only five.''

''You are not very old yourself.''

''I'm eight.''

''Well, you don't look it. Put him down I say!'' The old woman grabbed Long and set him on his feet. ''Now walk!''

Long burst into tears again. "We can't find Mama," he sobbed.

Mai put her arm around him. "We'll find her, Long. Be quiet. Help me listen for the bell. Shhhh!"

Long put both hands over his mouth and listened.

They did not hear the bell.

All day long they listened. . .and looked.

Finally the sun set behind the trees. It turned the sky into a rosy glow. Still they had not found Mama and baby Bao. The bent old woman limped beside them as she had done all day. Mai was glad she was with them.

At last, when it was too dark to go on, they stopped under a bush. The old woman stopped too. She fell asleep at once. So did Mai and Long.

It was much later when
Mai heard the tinkling of
Mama's bell. She jumped up
and ran to the side of the
road. "Mama! Mama!" she cried.
No one answered.
She listened and
called again. . . still, no one anwered.

The old woman crawled from under the bush
where she had been sleeping. "What is it, child?"

"I heard Mama's bell, but I don't see her."

"You must have been dreaming. Come back and
get some sleep. We need to be on the road early if we
are to reach the border by tomorrow night."

Slowly, Mai followed her back to the bush. "Help
us, please help us, God. . ." she prayed.

The next morning, the old woman walked very slowly. She seemed ill. Mai and Long stayed beside her. The crowds pushed past them.

After noon, Mai and Long took turns carrying the old woman's bundle. She seemed to grow weaker as the day wore on. At last, in the late afternoon she fell to the ground at the side of the road.

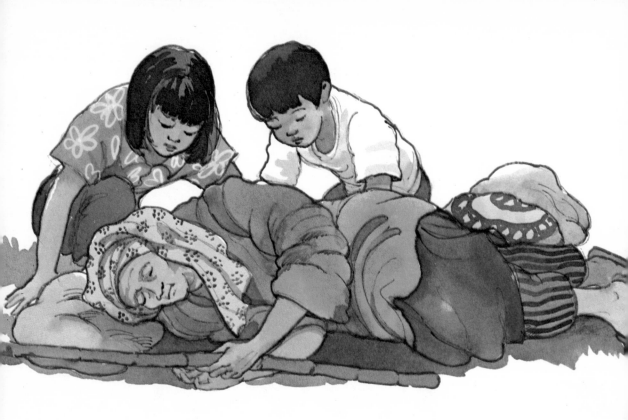

"Go on!" she cried, waving her cane. "Go on without me."

"We will not leave you," Mai said. "We will rest too, and then go on with you."

"I can't go any farther," the old woman said, shaking her head. "If you hurry, you can reach the border before dark. Go now. I can't make it."

"We have a little rice left. Will that help?"

"No. I won't eat your rice. You eat it. I will rest a while." She closed her eyes.

"What shall we do?" Long asked Mai.

"I don't know. I want to find Mama, but I don't want to leave the old one here. . . ."

"I'm tired too." Long dropped to the ground.

"So am I. Let's stay with her tonight. We can find a refugee camp in the morning."

"What about Mama?"

"We'll find her, Long. Don't worry. We'll find her and baby Bao."

Mai had been asleep what seemed only a short time when she heard Mama's bell. She started to get up but was sure she had been dreaming again. She noticed that the old woman was gone.

Then Mai heard the bell a second time.

Mai saw it was daylight. She was not dreaming. She jumped to her feet.

"Mama!" she cried.

In an instant her mother was kneeling beside her with baby Bao in her arms. "Mai! Long! You are safe! I found you!"

They hugged each other, crying with joy.

"How did you know we were here?" Mai asked.

"In the night, rescue workers came through the camp where I was. They were carrying an old woman on a stretcher. It seems they found her here last night when they were hunting for the sick and dying.

"When they brought her through the camp, she was very ill and weak. But when she heard my bell, she asked if I had lost you two. She told me where I could find you. I came as fast as I could. Thank the Lord I found you!"

"I knew we would find each other," Mai said, putting her arms around Mama.

"We asked the Lord to help us and He did, "Long added.

"I will thank Him every day, "Mama said. "Now let's get back to camp where it is safe."

And the four went happily down the road to the sound of the bell.